6 2184 52 5%

WALTHAM PUBLIC LIBRARY
3 4867 00511 9617

D1466065

WALTHAM PUBLIC LIBRARY

WALTHAM
PUBLIC LIBRARY

Bring Us Water, Molly Pitcher! ★

A Fun Song About the Battle of Monmouth

By Michael Dahl

Illustrated by Sandra D'Antonio

Special thanks to our advisers for their expertise:

Tom Mega, Ph.D., Department of History
University of St. Thomas (Minnesota)

Susan Kesselring, M.A., Literacy Educator
Rosemount–Apple Valley–Eagan (Minnesota) School District

PICTURE WINDOW BOOKS
MINNEAPOLIS, MINNESOTA

Managing Editor: Bob Temple
Creative Director: Terri Foley
Editor: Kristin Thoennes Keller
Editorial Adviser: Andrea Cascardi
Copy Editor: Laurie Kahn
Musical arrangement: Elizabeth Temple
Designer: Melissa Voda
Page production: The Design Lab
The illustrations in this book were created digitally.

Picture Window Books

**5115 Excelsior Boulevard
Suite 232
Minneapolis, MN 55416
1-877-845-8392
www.picturewindowbooks.com**

Copyright © 2004 by Picture Window Books
All rights reserved. No part of this book may be reproduced without written permission from
the publisher. The publisher takes no responsibility for the use of any of the materials or meth-
ods described in this book, nor for the products thereof.

Printed in the United States of America.

Library of Congress Cataloging-in-Publication Data
Dahl, Michael.
Bring us water, Molly Pitcher! : a fun song about the Battle of Monmouth / author, Michael
Dahl ; illustrator, Sandra D'Antonio.
p. cm. — (Fun songs)
Summary: Relates the Revolutionary War adventures of Mary Hays, called Molly Pitcher for
bringing fresh water to colonial troops during the Battle of Monmouth, interspersed with
verses of original song lyrics to be sung to the tune of "She'll Be Coming Around the Mountain."
ISBN 1-4048-0130-8 (lib. bdg.)
1. Monmouth, Battle of, Freehold, N.J., 1778—Juvenile literature. 2. Monmouth, Battle of,
Freehold, N.J., 1778—Songs and music—Juvenile literature. 3. Pitcher, Molly, 1754-1832—
Juvenile literature. 4. Pitcher, Molly, 1754-1832—Songs and music—Juvenile literature.
5. Women revolutionaries—United States—Biography—Juvenile literature. 6. Women
revolutionaries—United States—Songs and music—Juvenile literature. [1. Pitcher, Molly,
1754-1832. 2. Monmouth, Battle of, Freehold, N.J., 1778. 3. United States—History—
Revolution, 1775-1783—Campaigns. 4. Pitcher, Molly, 1754-1832—Songs and music. 5.
Monmouth, Battle of, Freehold, N.J., 1778—Songs and music. 6. United States—History—
Revolution, 1775-1783—Songs and music.] I. D'Antonio, Sandra, 1956- ill. II. Title.
E241.M7 D34 2004
973.3'082—dc21   2003009832

SING ONE! SING ALL!
It's the new historical ditty:
"Bring Us Water, Molly Pitcher!"

Sing along to the tune of "She'll Be Coming Around the Mountain."
Tell the tale of brave Mary Hays.
She helped win the Battle of Monmouth.
This was a hot battle in the American fight for freedom!

Many years ago, America was not a country. The states were called colonies. The people were called colonists. The King of Great Britain ruled them. He made them pay lots of money called taxes. The people did not think the taxes were fair.

Many colonists wanted to form their own country. They did not want to belong to Britain. These people were called patriots. They began to fight against the king's troops. But the king's army won most of the battles.

On June 28, 1778, the patriot army was running from the British army. But General George Washington said he was tired of running. He told his troops to take a stand. They lined up their cannons. They aimed at the British. One of the cannon gunners was William Hays. His wife Mary was at his side. She brought water to the troops. But she also ended up fighting! This song tells her story.

"Molly Pitcher! Bring us water when you come!
Molly Pitcher! Bring us water when you come!"

The day of the Battle of Monmouth was a hot one. Mary Hays brought fresh water to soldiers. They called her Molly Pitcher. Molly is a nickname for Mary.

"Molly Pitcher! Bring us water when you come!"

On this hot day, each cannon needed an hour to cool down. If they were not allowed to cool down, they would go off by accident.

Oh! The cannons crack
like thunder in the sun.
Oh! The cannons cook
like ovens in the sun.

9

More than three hundred men died at Monmouth. Many died from the heat.

Oh! The sun is hot as blazes.
A faint soldier up she raises.

Molly Pitcher lifts
that soldier in the sun.

"Molly Pitcher!
Your poor husband
has gone down!
Molly Pitcher!
Your poor husband
has gone down!

For a hidden British soldier
shot your William in the shoulder.

Molly Pitcher! Now he's lying
on the ground!"

"Oh! We've lost another rammer for our guns!
Oh! We've lost another rammer for our guns!

Wheel away the empty cannon since there's not another man in sight to ram the cannonballs in William's gun."

Molly takes the cannon's rammer in her hand! Molly takes the cannon's rammer in her hand!

"Load more balls and powder, fellas,
while those British cannons shell us.

Keep it coming!
William's gun will still be manned!"

That night, the Americans slept at their posts. They slept next to their guns and cannons. The British backed off. It was a patriot victory!

"Molly Pitcher!
Ram that cannon!
Ram that gun!
Molly Pitcher!
Ram that cannon!
Ram that gun!"

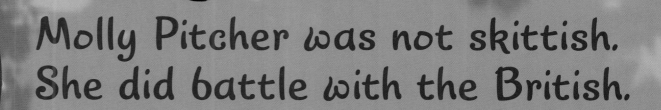

Molly Pitcher was not skittish.
She did battle with the British.

Molly Pitcher pitched
right in till it was won.

Bring Us Water, Molly Pitcher!

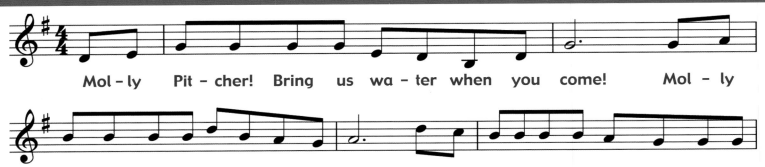

Mol – ly   Pit – cher!   Bring   us   wa – ter   when   you   come!   Mol – ly

Pit – cher! Bring us wa–ter when you come! We're as   dry as des–ert boul – ders, cry   the

hot and thir–sty sol – diers. Mol – ly   Pit – cher! Bring us   wa – ter when you come!

2. Oh! The cannons crack like thunder in the sun.
   Oh! The cannons cook like ovens in the sun.
   Oh! The sun is hot as blazes.
   A faint soldier up she raises.
   Molly Pitcher lifts that soldier in the sun.

3. Molly Pitcher! Your poor husband has gone down!
   Molly Pitcher! Your poor husband has gone down!
   For a hidden British soldier
   Shot your William in the shoulder.
   Molly Pitcher! Now he's lying on the ground!

4. Oh! We've lost another rammer for our guns!
   Oh! We've lost another rammer for our guns!
   Wheel away the empty cannon
   Since there's not another man in
   Sight to ram the cannonballs in William's gun.

5. Molly takes the cannon's rammer in her hand!
   Molly takes the cannon's rammer in her hand!
   Load more balls and powder, fellas,
   While those British cannons shell us.
   Keep it coming! William's gun will still be manned!

6. Molly Pitcher! Ram that cannon! Ram that gun!
   Molly Pitcher! Ram that cannon! Ram that gun!
   Molly Pitcher was not skittish.
   She did battle with the British.
   Molly Pitcher pitched right in till it was won.

Did You Know?

Did you know that a cannonball passed between Mary's legs? It could have killed her! One patriot soldier wrote about the war. His name was Joseph Plumb Martin. He wrote that the British soldiers aimed for Mary. Joseph saw a cannonball pass between her legs. It tore her skirt!

Mary Hays was a brave woman. She put up with the danger. She put up with the heat and noise. She kept working the cannon with her fellow patriots.

Did you know about the first Molly Pitcher? There was another woman who fought alongside her husband during battle. Her name was Margaret Corbin. She took over the cannon when her husband was killed. He died at Fort Washington in 1776. Margaret also was wounded in that battle.

GLOSSARY

cannon—a large gun that fires heavy metal balls

colonist—a person who lives in a new land but is ruled by people in a former land

patriot—a person who loves and fights for his or her country

pitcher—a holder for liquids; pitchers often have handles and spouts

tax—money that people pay to their government

To Learn More

AT THE LIBRARY

Parker, Lewis K. *The Battle of Monmouth*. San Diego: Blackbirch Press, 2002.

Rockwell, Anne F. *They Called Her Molly Pitcher*. New York: Alfred A. Knopf, 2002.

Ruffin, Frances E. *Molly Pitcher*. New York: PowerKids Press, 2002.

ON THE WEB

Molly Pitcher: US Field Artillery Association

http://www.usfaa.com/MollyPitcher

Offers details about Mary Hays's life

National Museum of American History

http://www.americanhistory.si.edu

Tells stories from American history
and includes hands-on activities

Fact Hound

Fact Hound offers a safe, fun way to find Web sites related to this book. All of the sites on Fact Hound have been researched by our staff.

http://www.facthound.com

1. Visit the Fact Hound home page.
2. Enter a search word related to this book or type in this special code: 1404801308.
3. Click on the FETCH IT button.

Your trusty Fact Hound will fetch the best sites for you!

WALTHAM
PUBLIC LIBRARY